Experiencing Chinese

国际语言研究与发展中心

Workbook
Elementary School

体验汉语®

练习册

小学

1

高等教育出版社
Higher Education Press

图书在版编目（CIP）数据

体验汉语小学练习册. 第1册 / 国际语言研究
与发展中心.—北京：高等教育出版社，2008.8
（2009重印）
ISBN 978-7-04-022270-8

Ⅰ.体… Ⅱ.国… Ⅲ.汉语−对外汉语教学−习题
Ⅳ.H195.4

中国版本图书馆CIP数据核字（2008）第119832号

策划编辑 周 芳 **责任编辑** 周 芳 **责任印制** 陈伟光

出版发行	高等教育出版社		**购书热线**	010-58581118
社 址	北京市西城区德外大街4号		**免费咨询**	800-810-0598
邮政编码	100120		**网 址**	http://www.hep.edu.cn
总 机	010-58581000			http://www.hep.com.cn
			网上订购	http://www.landraco.com
经 销	蓝色畅想图书发行有限公司			http://www.landraco.com.cn
印 刷	涿州市星河印刷有限公司		**畅想教育**	http://www.widedu.com
开 本	889×1194 1/16		**版 次**	2008年8月第1版
印 张	6.75		**印 次**	2009年4月第2次印刷
字 数	100 000			

本书如有印装等质量问题，请到所购图书销售部门调换。　ISBN 978-7-04-022270-8

目录

① **Read and write** 读读写写

ā

á

ǎ

à

āi

ái

ǎi

ài

āo

áo

ǎo

ào

án

ǎn

àn

ān

ǎng

āng

áng

àng

Listen and choose 听一听，选一选

1. ā āi

2. ǎo ǎn

3. áng àng

4. ái án

5. àn àng

6. āi āo

3 **Listen and number the pictures** 听录音，填序号

· gòu · gǒu

· māo · máo

· yú · yǔ

· niǎo · niào

☆ ☆ ☆ ☆ ☆

5 Choose and fill in the blanks 选择填空

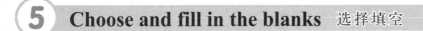

这 zhè   那 nà

___ shì (jī)

___ shì (niú)

___ shì (jī)

___ shì (niú)

1 Look and color　看一看，涂一涂

gǒu

māo

dàxiàng

xióngmāo

d	g	x	n
i	i	à	óng
x	ǒ	m	i
āo	ǎo	àng	u

3 Match 连一连

What is the animals' favorite food? Please match them.
这些动物最爱的食物是什么？请连一连。

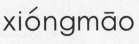
dàxiàng

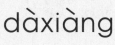
xióngmāo

māo

gǒu

niǎo

④ Walk and draw 走一走，画一画

After drawing all the pictures, you can find the exit.
要全部画完才能走出去哦！

Zhè shì dàxiàng.

Nà shì gǒu.

Zhè shì xióngmāo.

Nà shì niǎo.

Nà shì māo.

Zhè shì yú.

Chinese XP

5 Find sentences 找句子

nà	xióng	māo	niǎo	shì
māo	zhè	zhè	shì	gǒu
gǒu	nà	shì	gǒu	shì
zhè	yú	māo	dà	niǎo
niǎo	nà	shì	yú	xiàng

zhè shì māo

zhè shì gǒu

nà shì gǒu

nà shì yú

  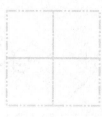    

① **Read and write**　读读写写

Chinese XP

ō

ǒ

ò

ó

òu

ǒu

ōu

òng

ǒng

óu

ōng

óng

Listen and mark the tones 听一听，写出声调

3 Listen and put a × mark on the syllables you hear
听录音，在听到的音节上画 ×

ó	ǒng	òu
ōu	ō	~~òng~~
ōng	óu	ǒu

Chinese XP®

l__sh__

__ué__eng

j___j___

_èi__ei

① **Listen and choose** 听一听，选一选

loǎshī

jěijei

xuéshegn

imèime

☆ ☆ ☆ ☆ ☆

3 Find and write 找一找，写一写

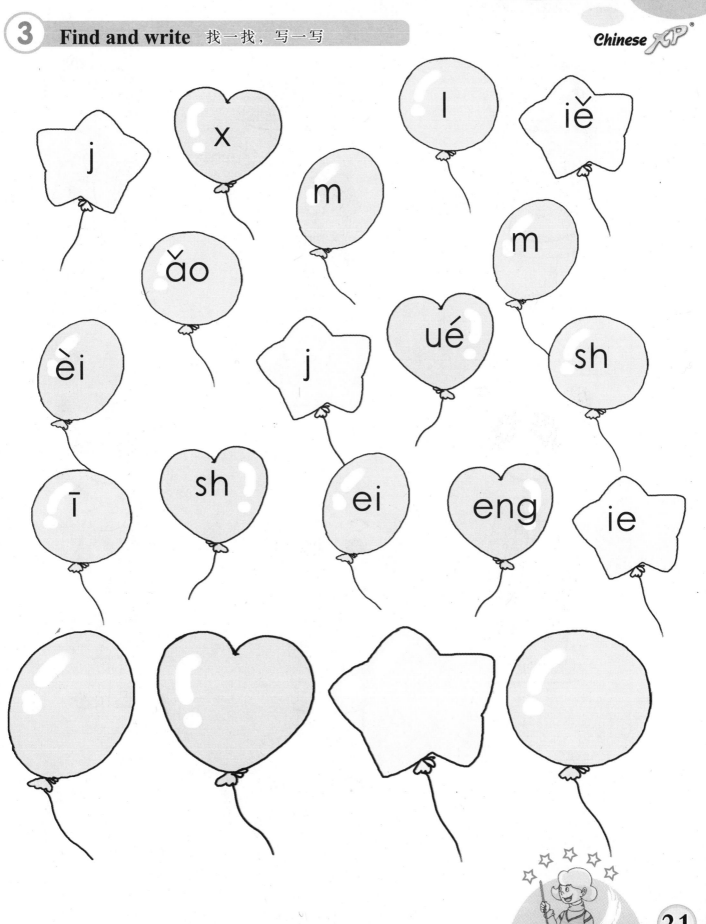

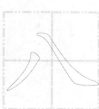
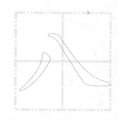
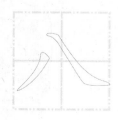
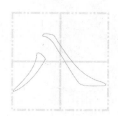

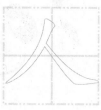
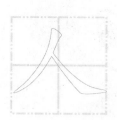
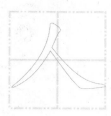

☆ ☆ ☆ ☆ ☆

① Read and write 读读写写

Chinese XP

ē

é

ě

è

ēi

éi

ěi

èi

ēn

ěn

èn

én

ēng

ěng

èng

ér

éng

èr

ēr

ér

ěr

☆☆☆☆☆

3 Listen and choose 听录音，选一选

1 ē   5 èn

2 ēi   6 èng

3 ěi   7 ér

4 én    8 ěr

5 Look and draw 看一看，画一画

According to the arrangement of the pictures, what should the picture be in the blanks?
根据图画的排列规律，空白处的图画应该是什么呢？

1

2

3

Match and draw 连一连，画一画

Dūyà

Měiměi

Měiměi de shàngyī.

Dūyà de shàngyī.

Měiměi de qúnzi.

Dūyà de kùzi.

1 Look and color　看一看，涂一涂

xié

qúnzi

màozi

shàngyī

wà+zi=

kù+zi=

qún+zi=

mào+zi=

☆☆☆☆☆

3 Find the differences 找不同

xié

kùzi

màozi

wàzi

Walk and draw 走一走，画一画

After drawing all the pictures, you can find the exit.
要全部画完才能走出去哦！

Tā de qúnzi.

Tā de xié.

Wǒ de wàzi.

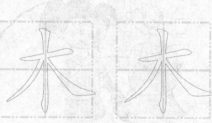

  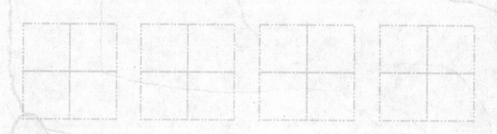

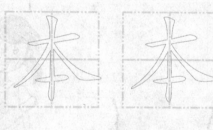

☆ ☆ ☆ ☆ ☆

① Read and write 读读写写

Chinese XP

yī

yí

yǎ

yì

iū

iú

iǔ

iù

iē

ié

iě

iè

īn

ín

ǐn

ìn

īng

ín

ǐng

ìng

Listen and circle 听一听，圈一圈

1. ī   ì

2. iù   ìn

3. iě   iǔ

4. ín   íng

5. ǐ   ǐn

6. iē   īn

3 **Count, write, and say** 数一数，写一写，说一说

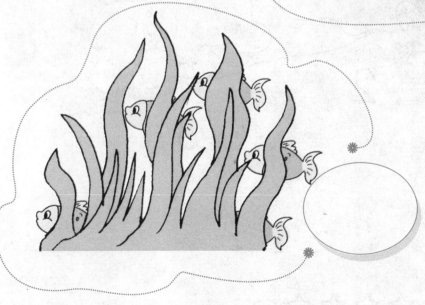

5 **Add and color** 加一加，涂一涂

$$7 + 1 = 8 \qquad 4 + (\ \ ) = 8$$

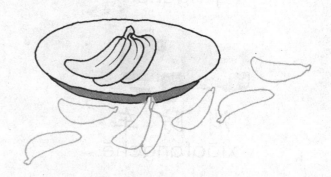

$$(\ \ ) + (\ \ ) = 8 \qquad (\ \ ) + (\ \ ) = 8$$

110

CHINA 中国

119

CHINA 中国

120

CHINA 中国

What are the emergency numbers in your country?

在你的国家，这些急救电话是多少？

警 车
jǐngchē

消 防 车
xiāofángchē

救 护 车
jiùhùchē

①　**Listen and match**　听一听，连一连

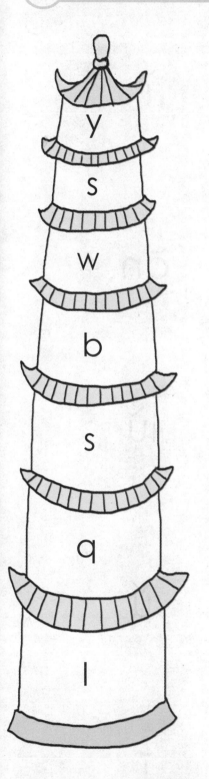

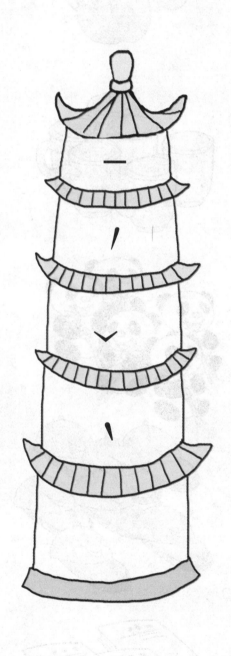

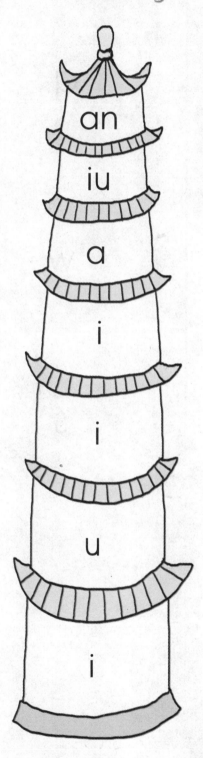

q

w

s

l

s

ì

ān

iù

ǔ

ī

☆☆☆☆☆

3 **Let's see who can find more cups, stools, and butterflys!**
看谁找到的多！

Chinese XP

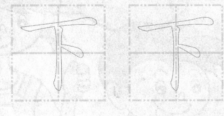  

① Read and write　读读写写

ū　ú　ǔ　ù
uī　uí　uǐ　uì
ūn　ǔn　ún　ùn

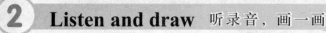

☆☆☆☆☆

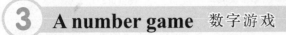

3 A number game 数字游戏

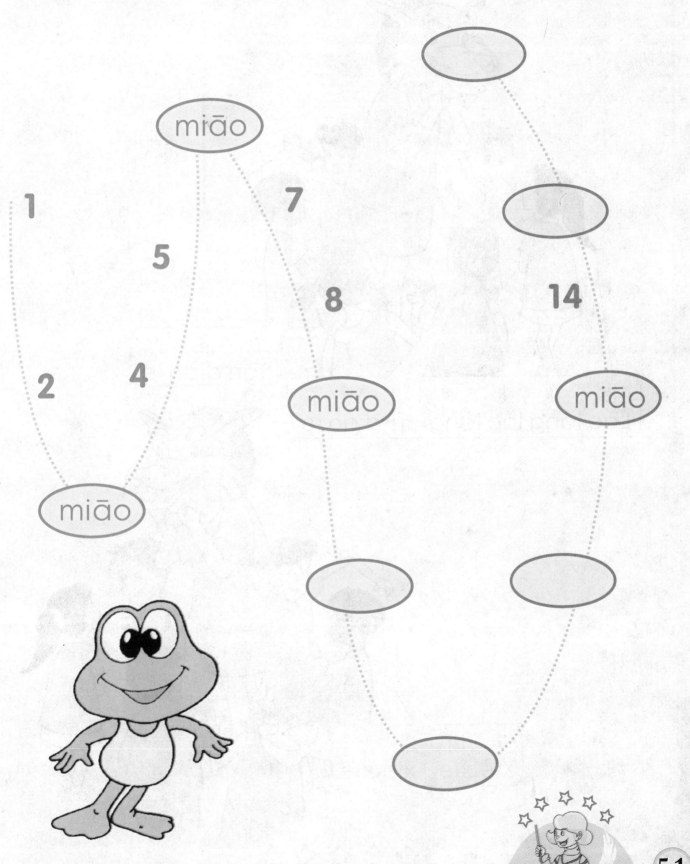

八点　　十一点　　七点　　两点

yī	èr	qī	sān
shí	yī	diǎn	sì
wǔ	liǎng	liù	qī
~~bā~~	~~diǎn~~	jiǔ	shí

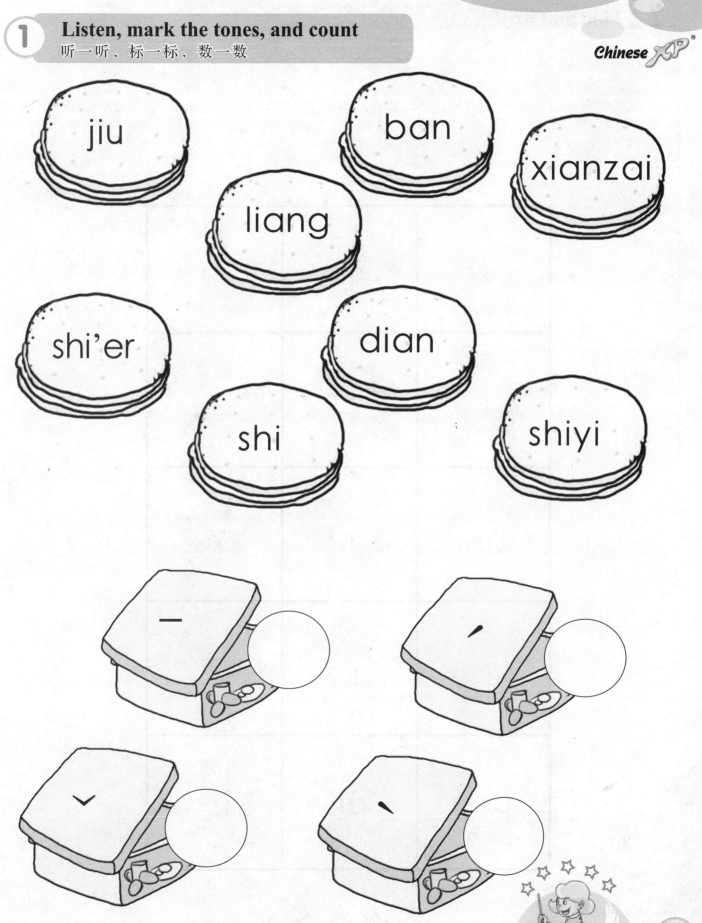

1 Listen, mark the tones, and count
听一听，标一标，数一数

jiu　ban　xianzai　liang　shi'er　dian　shi　shiyi

x	i	sh
í	j	i
àn	l	y
ī	i	z
ǎng	ài	ǔ

☆☆☆☆☆

3 **Match** 连一连

liǎng diǎn

jiǔ diǎn bàn

shí diǎn bàn

shí'èr diǎn

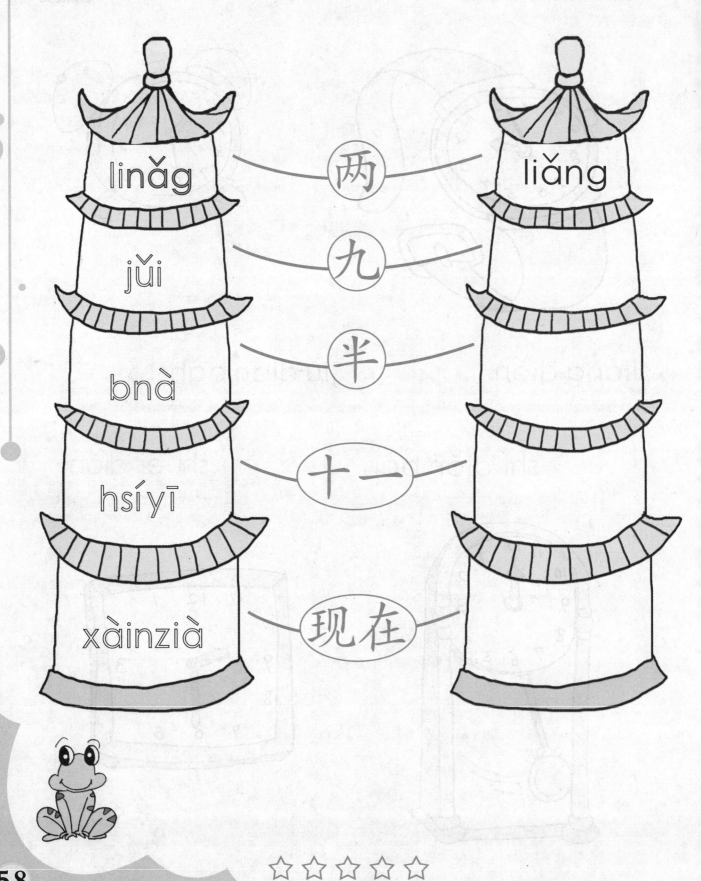

linǎg 两 liǎng

jǔi 九

bnà 半

hsíyī 十一

xàinzià 现在

5 **Look and write** 看一看，写一写

现 在 一 点 。
Xiànzài yī diǎn.

现 在 　　　点 。
Xiànzài 　　diǎn.

现 在
Xiànzài

1 Read and write　读读写写

ū

ú

ǔ

ù

yuē

yué

yuě

yuè

xuē

xué

xuě

xuè

yūn

yún

yǔn

yùn

1. ǜ   ú

2. yún   yú

3. xuē   yuē

4. ū   ū

5. xuè   yùn

6. ǔ   ǔ

☆ ☆ ☆ ☆ ☆

3 Listen, choose, and draw 听一听，选一选，画一画

1. ū　　　ú　　　ǔ　　　ù

2. ū　　　ú　　　ǔ　　　ù

3. (y)uē　　　　　(y)uě　　(y)uè

4. (y)ūn　　(y)ún　　(y)ǔn　　(y)ùn

wěiba

ěrduo

chìbǎng

yǎnjing

jiǎo

Chinese XP

5 **Look and draw** 看一看，画一画

According to the arrangement of the pictures, what the picture should be in the blanks?
根据图画的排列规律，空白处的图画应该是什么呢？

1  _____

2 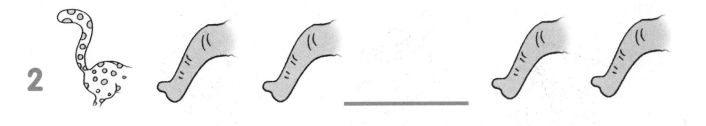 _____

3 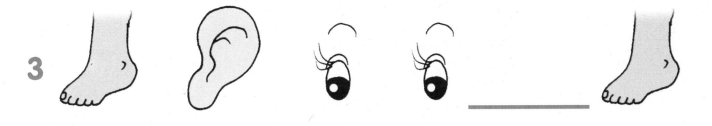 _____

4  _____

我 有 妹妹。
Wǒ yǒu mèimei.

猫 有 帽子。
Māo yǒu màozi.

她 有 鞋。
Tā yǒu xié.

1 **Finish the pictures and color the *Pinyin*** 画一画，描一描

yǎnjing

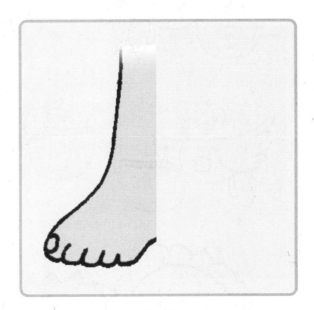

jiǎo

wěiba

chìbǎng

3 **Match** 连一连

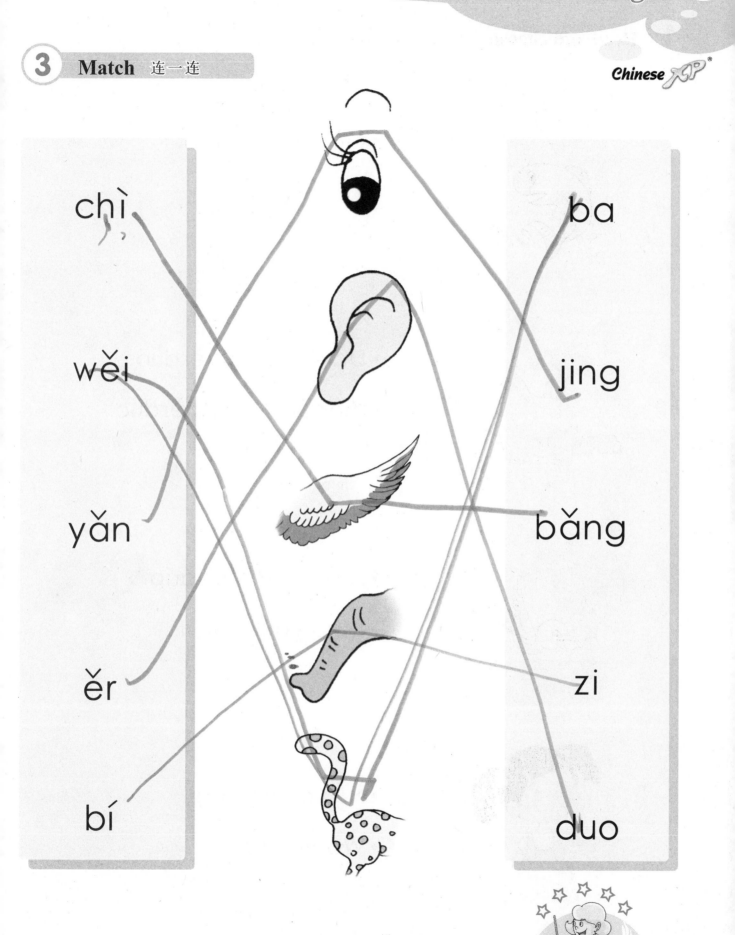

chì

wěi

yǎn

ěr

bí

ba

jing

bǎng

zi

duo

- Gǒu yǒu wěiba.
- Yú yǒu wěiba.

- Dàxiàng yǒu ěrduo.
- Xióngmāo yǒu ěrduo.

- Niǎo yǒu chìbǎng.
- Māo yǒu wěiba.

- Nǐ yǒu yǎnjing.
- Wǒ yǒu bízi.

⑤ Look and count 看一看，数一数

Chinese XP®

几个动物有翅膀？
How many animals have wings?

几个动物有尾巴？
How many animals have tails?

几个动物有脚？
How many animals have feet?

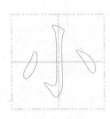 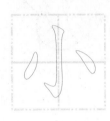  

☆ ☆ ☆ ☆ ☆

1 **Read and write** 读读写写

m

f

p

b

n

t

d

h

t

g

k

ai·s

p

pa   pai   pan

m

ma   mai   man

b

ba   bai   ban

d

di   din   ding

t

ti   tin   ting

l

li   lin   ling

g

ge   gen   geng

k

ke   ken   keng

☆☆☆☆☆

3 Listen and choose 听录音，选一选

ài èi ǎo ǒu ài ào iè üè

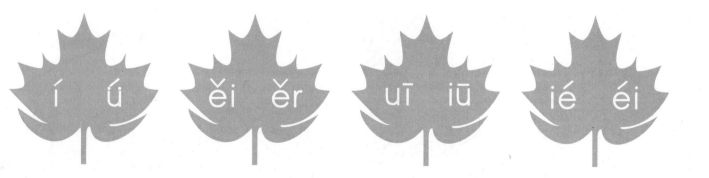

í ú ěi ěr uī iū ié éi

Color and say 涂一涂，说一说

báisè

lùsè   lánsè

huángsè   hēisè

hóngsè

1 **Listen and match** 听一听，连一连

l

b

h

一

ˊ

ˇ

ˋ

ai

ü

ei

an

ong

uang

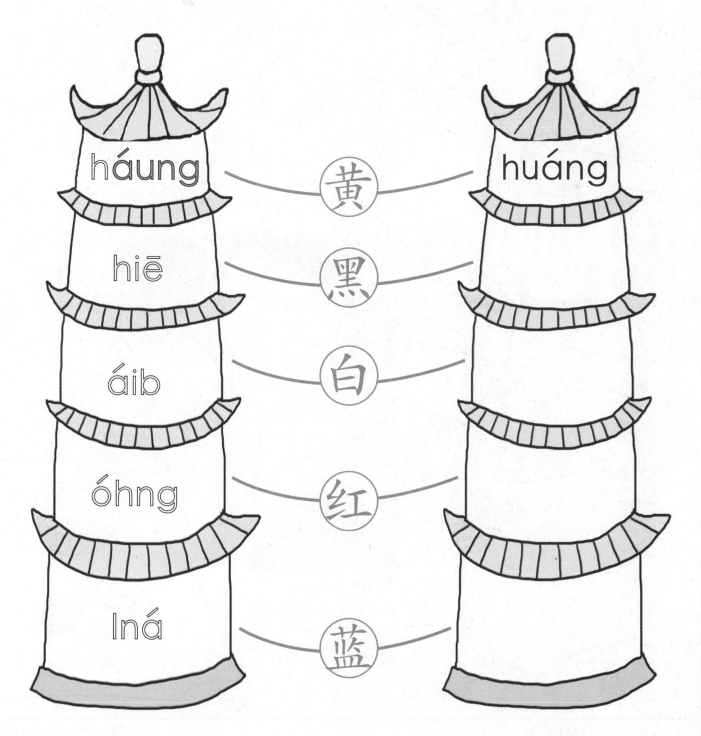

3 **Color the wrong parts of the _Pinyin_ and correct them** 涂一涂，改一改

háung   黄   huáng

hiē   黑

áib   白

óhng   红

lná   蓝

Look and number the parts of the picture 看一看，填序号

1. báisè   **2.** lùsè   **3.** hóngsè

4. lánsè   **5.** huángsè

☆ ☆ ☆ ☆ ☆

1 **Read and write** 读读写写

j

q

x

z

r

zh

c

w

y

s

ch

sh

j

ji　jin　jing

q

qi　qin　qing

z

za　zai　zan

c

ca　cai　can

r

re　ren　reng

zh

zhe　zhen　zheng

w

wu　wan　wang

y

yi　yan　yang

3 **Listen and choose** 听录音，选一选

Chinese XP

1. í   ū   uī   iū

2. ái   án   àng   áo

3. iē   iū   īn   ī

4. ān   ēn   āng   ēng

5. ǐ   ǐn   ǐng   ěng

6. ài   èi   uì   iè

这是······   zhè shì······

5 **Find and count** 找一找，数一数

māma 妈妈

nǎinai 奶奶

奶	妹	妹	姐	妹
姐	妈	妹	妈	妈
妹	妈	奶	姐	妈
姐	奶	姐	奶	妹
姐	妹	妹	奶	奶

6 A chick looks for mom 小鸡找妈妈

妈 妈
māma

① **Listen and color** 听一听，涂一涂

bàba

yéye

gūgu

gēge

shěnshen

shūshu

jiějie

jiùjiu

mèimei

dìdi

nǎinai

māma

Find and write 找一找，写一写

nǎinai

y	n	d	m
ì	ā	é	d
y	ǎi	i	m
ai	a	e	n

3 Color the pictures and *Pinyin* 涂一涂

nǎinai

māma

yéye

bàba

nǎinai

bàba

yéye

māma

dìdi

gēge

5 **Match and find the same parts** 连一连，找相同

爸　爸　　grandma

爷　爷　　mom

奶　奶　　grandpa

妈　妈　　dad

95

96

☆ ☆ ☆ ☆ ☆

第1课 动物

2. 听一听，选一选

1. ā 2. ǎn 3. áng 4. ái 5. àn 6. āo

3. 听录音，填序号

4 3 6 5 1 2

录音文本：
1. 这是大象。 2. 那是鸟。 3. 那是猫。
4. 这是鱼。 5. 这是熊猫。 6. 那是狗。

4. 选一选

gǒu māo yú niǎo

5. 选择填空

zhè nà nà zhè

6. 这是什么？

xiong mao   da xiang

第2课 这是狗

2. 找一找，写一写

gǒu   niǎo   dàxiàng   xióngmāo

3. 连一连

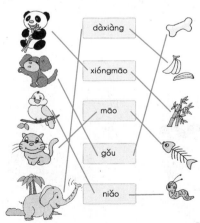

5. 找句子

nà	xióng	māo	niǎo	shì
māo	zhè	zhè	shì	gǒu
gǒu	nà	shì	gǒu	shì
zhè	yú	māo	dà	niǎo
niǎo	nà	shì	yú	xiàng

第3课 人物

2. 听一听，写出声调

‾ ´ ` ` ` ´ ´ `

录音文本：
1. ō 2. ǒu 3. òng 4. ǒng
5. óu 6. ó 7. ōng 8. òu

3. 听录音，在听到的音节上画×。

òng ǒng ōu óu ō

4. 他们是谁？

他们是白雪公主和七个小矮人。

她是美人鱼。   他是学生。

他是圣诞老人。   她是老师。

5. 看一看，写一写

lǎoshī xuésheng jiějie mèimei

第4课　她是妹妹

1. 听一听，选一选
　　1. wǒ　　2. tā　　3. nǐ　　4. xuésheng
　　5. lǎoshī　　6. jiějie

2. 改一改，涂一涂
　　loǎshī —— lǎoshī　　jěijei —— jiějie
　　xuéshegn —— xuésheng
　　imèime —— mèimei

3. 找一找，写一写

mèimei　　　　　　xuésheng

jiějie　　　　　　lǎoshī

4. 猜一猜，写一写

Wǒ shì Jiékè.　Wǒ shì Dūyà.　Wǒ shì Fēn.

Wǒ shì Tíngting.　Wǒ shì Mèiměi.　Wǒ shì Dīngding.

第5课　衣服

2. 听一听，涂一涂
　　1. ēn　2. ě　3. ēi　4. éi　5. è　6. é

3. 听录音，选一选

1 　　2 　　3 　　4

5 　　6 　　7 　　8

5. 看一看，画一画

第6课　我的鞋

2. 写一写，连一连
　　wàzi　kùzi　qúnzi　màozi

3. 找不同

第7课　数字

2. 听一听，圈一圈
　　1. ī　2. ìn　3. iǔ　4. íng　5. ǐ　6. iē

3. 数一数，写一写，说一说

2　　　　　　7

8

5

4. 哪条路最近?
第3条路

5. 加一加，涂一涂
7+1=8 4+4=8 5+3=8 3+5=8

第8课 数一数

1. 听一听，连一连
wǔ yī sì sān liù bā qī

2. 数一数，连一连

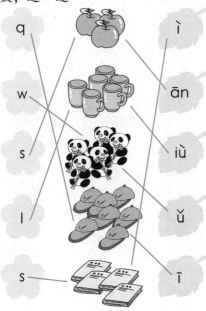

3. 看谁找到的多!

 5   5   4

第9课 时间

2. 听录音，画一画

录音文本：
1. 现在两点。   2. 现在九点。
3. 现在六点。   4. 现在三点半。
5. 现在七点半。   6. 现在十一点半。

3. 数字游戏
10 11 miāo miāo 16

5. 找一找

yī	èr	qī	sān
shí	yī	diǎn	sì
wǔ	liǎng	liù	qī
bā	diǎn	jiǔ	shí

第10课   现在两点

1. 听一听，标一标，数一数
jiǔ liǎng bàn xiànzài shí'èr
shí diǎn shíyī
（ˉ）1个   （ˊ）3个
（ˇ）3个   （ˋ）4个

2. 找一找，写一写

liǎng   jiǔ   xiànzài   shíyī

4. 涂一涂，改一改
　　linǎg —— liǎng　　jǔi —— jiǔ
　　bnà —— bàn　　hsíyī —— shíyī
　　xàinzià —— xiànzài

5. 看一看，写一写

　　现在一点。　　Xiànzài yī diǎn.
　　现在两点。　　Xiànzài liǎng diǎn.
　　现在三点半。　　Xiànzài sān diǎn bàn.
　　现在四点。　　Xiànzài sì diǎn.
　　现在八点半。　　Xiànzài bā diǎn bàn.
　　现在十点半。　　Xiànzài shí diǎn bàn.

第11课　身体

2. 听一听，在听到的拼音前画√
　　1. ù　2. yún　3. xuē　4. ū　5. yùn　6. ǔ

3. 听一听，选一选，画一画
　　1. ǔ　2. ú　3. (y)uè　4. (y)ún

4. 连一连，说一说

　　wěiba
　　ěrduo
　　chìbǎng
　　yǎnjing
　　jiǎo

5. 看一看，画一画

6. 看一看，选一选

第12课　鸟有翅膀

2. 找一找，数一数
　　y（2）　　　z（3）　　　uo（2）
　　b（9）　　　ei（4）　　　i（8）

3. 连一连

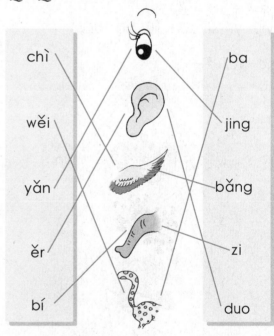

　　chì　　　　　　　ba
　　wěi　　　　　　　jing
　　yǎn　　　　　　　bǎng
　　ěr　　　　　　　zi
　　bí　　　　　　　duo

4. 读一读，选一选
　　·Yú yǒu wěiba.
　　·Dàxiàng yǒu ěrduo.
　　·Niǎo yǒu chìbǎng.
　　·Wǒ yǒu bízi.

5. 看一看，数一数
　　几个动物有翅膀？（1个）
　　几个动物有尾巴？（5个）
　　几个动物有脚？(5个)

第13课 颜色

3. 听录音，选一选。
1. èi   2. ǒu   3. ào   4. iè
5. ú   6. ěr   7. iū   8. éi

第14课   我喜欢红色

1. 听一听，连一连
1. hēi   2. huáng   3. lán
4. bái   5. hóng   6. lù

2. 找一找，写一写

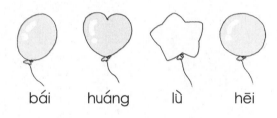

bái   huáng   lù   hēi

3. 涂一涂，改一改
háung —— huáng   hiē —— hēi
áib —— bái   óhng —— hóng
lná —— lán

第15课   家人

3. 听录音，选一选
1. ū   2. áo   3. ī   4. ēng   5. ǐng   6. uì

5. 找一找，数一数
妈妈（4） 奶奶（5）

第16课   我爱妈妈

1. 听一听，涂一涂
1. 妈妈 māma   2. 爷爷 yéye
3. 奶奶 nǎinai   4. 哥哥 gēge
5. 爸爸 bàba   6. 弟弟 dìdi

2. 找一找，写一写

nǎinai   māma   yéye   dìdi

4. 看一看，选一选

nǎinai   bàba   yéye

māma   dìdi   gēge

5. 连一连，找相同
爸爸 —— dad   爷爷 —— grandpa   父
奶奶 —— grandma   妈妈 —— mom   女

郑 重 声 明